Sodomy Is Not Enough!

Ribald Rhymes
&
Other Verse

Sodomy Is Not Enough!

Ribald Rhymes
&
Other Verse

Clive Murphy

To John & Ann with very best wishes — & thank you for subscribing!

Clive,
7/2/08

Brick Lane Books
London

Published in 2008 by Brick Lane Books
132 Brick Lane, London E1 6RU
Tel: +44 (020) 7247 6626
Website: www.clivemurphy.org

ISBN: 978-0-9541563-3-6

Copyright © Clive Murphy 2008

British Library Cataloguing in Publication Data
A catalogue record for this book is
available from The British Library

Cover illustration by Gary Parkinson
Cover photograph by Ken Pridmore

Printed in Great Britain

Headings and text set in
Times New Roman

Distributed by the Publisher

By the same author

Fiction:

SUMMER OVERTURES
FREEDOM FOR MR MILDEW
NIGEL SOMEONE

Verse:

SOUR GRAPES (illustrated)
CAVE CANEM
ORTS AND ALL
LUST AND MALICE

Autobiographies, recorded and edited by Clive Murphy:

THE GOOD DEEDS OF A GOOD WOMAN
The Memoirs of an East End hostel-dweller
BEATRICE ALI

BORN TO SING
The Memoirs of an East End mantle presser
ALEXANDER HARTOG

FOUR ACRES AND A DONKEY
The Memoirs of a lavatory attendant
S.A.B. ROGERS

LOVE, DEARS!
The Memoirs of a former chorus girl
MARJORIE GRAHAM

OIKY
The Memoirs of a pigman
LEN MILLS

AT THE DOGS IN DULWICH
The Memoirs of a poet
PATRICIA DOUBELL

A STRANGER IN GLOUCESTER
The Memoirs of an Austrian in England
MRS FALGE-WAHL

A FUNNY OLD QUIST
The Memoirs of a gamekeeper
EVAN ROGERS

DODO
The Memoirs of a left-wing socialist
DODO LEES

ENDSLEIGH
The Memoirs of a river-keeper
HORACE ADAMS

In preparation:

APRIL FOOL
The Memoirs of a former prep school headmaster
EVAN HOPE-GILL

ANGEL OF THE SHADOWS
The Memoirs of a cat lady
JOAN LAUDER

STREET PEOPLE
The Memoirs of a transsexual
ANGELLA DEE SHERRIFF, formerly David A. Sherriff

For
John Hallier and Joanna Dickens

CONTENTS

The Ugly Snail

Came out.

Looked about;

Met beauteous competition.

Returned to shell,

A lonely hell,

Lamenting his condition.

Ain't life absurd!

To a hungry bird

Now taking up position,

Out or in

Or ugly as sin

A snail just means nutrition.

Liberace
to Rubinstein's Promoter

"Tell me what the fact is.

Does Artur *never* practise?"

Spoilt Adolescent
Demands Room Service
at The Connaught Hotel

"I'm the son of Sir James McPhee.

Behave towards me inappropriately.

I acquired the habit when only three,

Sitting on my father's knee.

Don't delay. Don't be coy.

Don't tell me that I'm just a boy.

Should you deny my principal joy,

I'll stay instead at The Savoy."

Punning Metaphysical

"My youth I spent much underdone*.

Somewhat 'Cymbeline', Act lll, Scene l."

* under Donne

Sodomy Is Not Enough!

I wouldn't mind

But he never gets beyond behind.

Bibestiality

"Stallion or mare?"

"The pair."

Introducing Herself in a Tone of Hauteur, the Queen of the Fairies is Met by Lower Class Impudence

"My name is Titania."

"Well, that'll larn ya!"

Liar

"Do I do *what*?!
I do not."

Aesthete

He'll only show it
To a poet.

Cock Fright

It grew and grew
And then it *crew*!!

Thank Heaven for Little Boys
(with apologies to Alan Jay Lerner)

Thank heaven for little boys!

For little boys get bigger every day.

Thank heaven for little boys!

They grow up in the most delightful way.

That winkle shell so helpless and appealing

One day, full cock, will send you rocking

through the ceiling.

Thank heaven for little boys!

Thank heaven for them all,

No matter where, no matter who.

Without them what would little goys do?

Thank heaven ...

Thank heaven ...

Thank heaven for little boys!

Paranoid Heterosexual MP On Finding Himself in a Gay Ambience

Made hasty retreat.

Afraid for his seat.

Edelweiss

Hans turned to ice

When I sang "Idle Vice"

As we lolled making love in the station.

"Board the next train!

Never touch me again! ..."

That Kraut hates mis*pro*nunciation.

The Arrow

"How can you worship someone *quite* so

stupid?!"

"Consult Cupid."

Latin and Greek
or
The Long and the Short of It

Homo, homo -

Long o, short o:

Man or male, the same.

The hoi polloi don't get them right.

Classicists, put up a fight!

Protect your name!

Nonsense Rhyme

A man outside a bell tent
Was standing on his head.
I asked him why. He answered,
"My feet, they feel like lead."

Another, dressed in Fair Isle,
Had brows that he was knitting.
I asked him why. He answered,
"Because my head is splitting."

A third, crazed and erratic,
A Persian (blind) was sucking.
I asked him why. He answered,
"Your mind own business fucking!"

The Only Gayboy
of the Western World

My cock is like a cobra.
My sperm is thick as Brie.
My arse is sweet and juicy -
Fuck it now. Feel free.

I ride like an Atilla.
My hair waves like a tree.
But I crook my little finger
When I'm drinking tea.

My pecs are round as hillocks.
My balls weigh to my knee,
But if you call them pillocks
You're far too rough for me.

Yah boo sucks! I'm Christy Mahon!
Yah boo sucks! I'm Christy Mahon!
Yah boo sucks! I'm Christy Mahon!
You're far too rough for me.

Irish Plasterer
and
His English Mate

"Get off me back, young bucko!"
"I can't, old chap. I'm stucco."

Passive Muslim Tourist
Goes from Brothel to Brothel

Earl's Court, Bayswater, Soho ...

His holiday plan

Is to take in as much as he possibly can

Of man after man after man after man

From sunset to sunrise. It's Ramadan.

Watching out for Paedophiles

We are Vigil Aunties.
Be careful what you think.
If we believe your mind's on kids,
We want you in the clink.

My name is Hysteria,
Mine is Keyhole Kate.
Mine is Mrs.Grundy ...
We patrol the Internate.

We're even spying on the beach
To catch you stare or peep.
By God, it's fun. We take the *Sun*
While round the sand we creep.

We'll track you to a foreign town,
Assume your motives rotten.
Then, noncified by Wig and Gown,
You'll be locked up, forgotten.

You reason you are aesthetes pure.

You claim you're seeking knowledge.

Innocents from Neverland?

You'll soon be doing porridge.

We are Vigil Aunties.

To witch-hunt is our game.

Molester, non-molester -

The adrenalin's the same.

But if molesting *is* your trick,

If children give your only kick,

Take these tips from us:

To avoid a hellish long-term nick,

Top yourself with a blunderbuss

Or bury your victims quick.

The Usual Histoire

Blum, Blum,

The Piper's son.

Why did he steal?

Why did he run?

For a butcher in Lille.

Cherchez l'homme.

Stylite -April, 2006

The Reverend Foley,

Ever so holy,

Is missing his curate in Lent

So, though it's a killer,

He's sat on a pillar

To punish himself and repent.

Sciatica

"If you're into taboos in Great Britain
(I'm talking of sexual bent);
If it's No-zones by which you are smitten,
Sciatica comes Heaven-sent.

All praise to her rack and her biting.
All praise to the curse of her gnaw.
They're better than being in Queer Street,
Enduring the spite of the Law.

Sciatica cuts out your craving.
Sciatica spares you from guilt.
Sciatica keep you behaving.
Sciatica makes your cock wilt.

So don't seek a cure from your doctor.
Don't let him prescribe you Deep Sound.
Foster your Darling Sciatica,
Sing, "Love you to death. Stick around."

How to Bamboozle
a Psychologist

"Please explain this paradox:

I have wet nightmares when in socks."

One of those Mistakes

Thought he was winking, flashed my dick.

Discovered he'd a nervous tic.

Nostalgia

"Gin and orange?! The nancy boy's fish and
chips!"

Like we were told ballet is poofs' football.

The nagging barrage was relentless;

We resented it.

There were suicides,

Yet, sticks and stones,

The rest of us dressed nicely,

Minded our manners,

Didn't swear:

We were humble.

And secrecy had its thrill.

The Game of Billiards

Agent of doom,
He let them use the Billiard Room.
One infected,
Neither protected,
In a drunken haze
They lay on the beize
Of his Billiard Room.
A bed is a bed, a quilt is a quilt;
Rooms should be used for the reasons
                              they're built.
So why will nothing assuage his guilt?

Sexual Terrorists

In decay,
Knowing their own death beckons anyway,
And, without protection,
Bequeathing to others their own deadly infection...
All things considered, I find I have to say:
"Give me your commoner garden suicide
                              bomber any day."

Peace in Time of War

Off base. Under the stars. Within the Medina.
"Dear boy, another kiss!"
Once, in their ways, they'd have thought
this Decadence, Damnation, The Abyss ...
Yet, tonight, the encounter is a Benison,
a passing to Heartsease from the Infernal:
Each freed, transfigured - the redneck
rookie and his diehard colonel.

Cosmonautical Intimacy

"Let's call it a day
In the Milky Way."

A Roman Catholic
With After-The-Ball Blues

I gave a party (stag) tonight,

The best I've ever given.

The best for my guests. They left in pairs,

But I'm alone, unshriven.

Zip Level

I'm sitting in a Tube train. It's between

    Mile End and Bow.

Three men are standing, facing me.

    They're standing in a row.

Why are my cheeks reddening? (I feel

    them all-aglow.)

Contentment. Public pleasure. I came out

    long ago.

Male Prostitute Spends the Night with Repellent Captain of the Preservative Industry

Present sorrow.

Jam tomorrow.

Easy Twenty-Two Year Old Entices Potential Sugar Daddy

"Mine died before I was ever a lad.

Please be the father I never had -

Or who never had me, which is equally sad."

The Non-Smoker

There was a young fellow from Woking

Sucked cocks to prevent him from smoking.

The badge on his sweater

Said BIGGER IS BETTER:

He died of fellatial choking.

Bobby Shafto
Lies to Suspicious Future Wife
on His Return

"Sex abaft

On the craft?

Don't be so daft!"

Ex-Actor

Stopped fakin'.

Now forsaken.

Eve Being Hurtfully Humorous After Falling in the Garden

"Your Red Hot Poker

Is mediocre."

Ruthless Sun-Worshipper

With my body I thee worship;

Under thee I sweat.

Then this blinking bloke arrives

Upon my virtue set.

With my body I thee worship;

Under thee I spread.

Then this blinking bloke arrives.

Oh, how I see red!

With my body I thee worship;

For thee alone I bake.

Then this blinking bloke arrives

Again, for heaven's sake!

With my body I thee worship;

Under thee I stretch.

Then this blinking bloke arrives

To wank me off, the wretch.

With my body I thee worship;

Under thee I soak.

Then this blinking bloke arrives

Insisting on a poke.

Thou a furnace; I a candle,

In Earthly terms as hot to handle,

I let their fingers burn.

Thou know'st that unto thee for ever,

After what and whomsoever,

I always return.

Linked Abbreviations

DIY

MEANZ

RSI

The Oh-So-Knowing Shop Girl

She stares so smirkily
Above those tits,
Yet the slap he buys
Is to hide his zits.

Would He Have Behaved Differently Had I Said I Was Irish?

"Let me toss your caber

After tearing off that kilt!

I've travelled to the Highlands

To learn how Scots are built."

"Another Sassenach!" he snarled.

"Another same-sex lecher!"

I never learned how he was built.

I'm lying on a stretcher.

But I don't regret my forwardness.

I'm always playing Puck.

A chance is a fine thing, they say,

And you never know your luck.

Obliging Others

John likes me in a pirate patch.

For Brad it's 'transferred' knees.

Phil, baubles woven through my thatch;

Bert, scarlet eyelids please.

Jamal ordains a penis white,

Abe chains of malachite ...

They dropped round for group sex tonight.

I felt I looked a sight.

Patronising Earl While Being Penetrated with Difficulty by a Viscount

"I call this 'widening my social circle' -

Rather like reading Angela Thirkell."

Bill Must Have Quiet to Operate

"Oh, yes, Bill! Yes, yes, *yes*, Bill!

Flow to fill my cup!"

"I will, I will, I *will*, Will.

But, first, would you shut up!"

Personal Ad. Inserted in 'The Stage' by Finicky Theatrical Dresser (Retired)

Must be effete

With provocative seat

And a packet that's neat.

And please don't reply

If you don't ever cry

And haven't played Buttons or Pete*.

*Peter Pan

The word gay now means
"rubbish" in modern
playground speak ...
The Times 6.6.06

"Backlash.

Norms under threat.

'Trash',

'666', even, to come yet.

Bruvver,

Take cover!"

More Than I Bargained For

"I do apologise Mr. Drewitt.

Nothing on earth would make me do it.

Please stay calm, try not to flip.

I thought you just needed companionship."

The Poet Cannot Think of an Appropriate Name that Rhymes

"They call me Lolly.

I drive a truck.

I'm sweet by nature:

I let them suck.

I often wonder

As they dive and duck

What they'd call me

If I let them fuck."

31

The Quark

Is it a quark that moves from here to
　　there and yon, without appearing
　　to cross the intervening spaces?
If so, fair Keith is the quark of park and
　　heath and all such places.
At first, he lies beside you, then he's
　　gone to where another face is,
Accepting affection in the long grasses
　　of each new oasis,
Enwrapped, enraptured, but fleetingly, by
　　our welcoming embraces.

Gay Epitaph - Chiseller Loses All Control

UNDER THIS SOD LIES MR. SMEE.

UNDER A SOD'S WHERE I'D LIKE TO BE.

Young Greenheart and World-Weary Monster

Met him in a Heathrow loo

Before he flew to Kalamazoo.

Liked him. Shed a tear. Boohoo.

"So noo [new]!" he sneered. He was cabin crew.

In Vino Veritas

"You've been so loyal down the years."

"Cheaper than using brothels. Cheers!"

Out of the Closet - And How!

So careful he was we shouldn't rumble him,

It took an hour for Dad to tumble him.

He then announced with a peal of laughter,

"Father for lunch. The main meal after."

Two Knights Jousting

"You call yourself a Sybaritic Knight.

I thought that *I* was one until tonight.

I must, though, be a Sybarite Not Quite.

Jousting non-stop's a bit much for me.

Let's break for bickies and a cup of tea."

How to Handle a Racist

"Does your pulse beat faster when
blackies draw near?"
"Yes. Libidinal arousal, not fear, my dear."

Mean American Tourist (Male) Encounters Reasonably Priced Tart (Male) in London's Old Compton Street

"What do you seek in this 'street of vice'?"

"Puppy-dogs' tails and all that's nice."

"What else do you seek in this 'street of shame'?"

"The libido I lose when I'm with a dame."

"Anything more in this 'merry hell'?"

"Sexual madness under your spell."

"I'm forty-five quid - that's plus kip and a lie-in."

"And I'm Mr. Loaded! No harm in trying!"

35

How to Insult a Prospective Bedfellow

"Put a mask on

And don't last long."

World Cup Defeat

Yob, yob, yob.

Hear how they sob!

Their heroes run after a ball for a living:

You'd think it was lives in Iraq they were giving.

I'm a snob.

But I Secretly Rather Admire This Deprived Kid from Dublin Who's Trying to Pull Himself Up Socially by His Own Bootstraps

"The coffee has got to be Turkish;
The opera mustn't be 'slight';
One can't be seen folding a napkin.
Pity your vowels aren't right.

'Fungi' should be 'of this morning',
Silver not overly bright,
Pasta precisely al dente.
Pity your lipstick's a sight.

You won't be yourself for a jiffy:
You're always so bloody polite.
You once, kid, were Pride of the Liffey.
Don't buy your knickers so tight!"

A Particularly Sad Poem

At a sauna the other day,

Brian was snubbed in every way.

When he asked why, no one would say.

Homophobia

He tries to punch me.

I feint. He hits the wall.

I invite him home to apply ice.

No dice,

But he's now apoplectically *up* that wall

And I am standing ten feet tall.

Two Questions

1

If gay men had to have a bust,

About its size would they be fussed?

2

Why are heteros rarely any good

At explaining the workings of the

 lower female anatomy as heteros should?

Saturday Night in Surbiton

"Quick!! Smash more Ming against the wall,
Shout, 'Naked, you are beyond riches -
And comeliest of all!'!!"

Royalty

"I love you," I whispered, "more than
    anything in the whole wide world."
His lip curled.
"How do you mean 'any*thing*'?!!
I am your *King*!!"
And a Royal Banner he unfurled.

Gordon Ramsay*

Does Mr. Ramsay swear so much at home

Or suffer from Tourette's TV Syndrome?

* The celebrated chef and restaurateur

Straight Talk of 'Bender' to a Condescending 'Straight'

"Bit of skirt.

In; squirt;

Baby,

Maybe.

In your honour why need I metaphorically

kneel?

What's the big deal?"

The Courteous Rapist

"Sorry, I'm *so* sorry, Murray.

Train to catch. In a hurry."

Gnomic Utterances

"Who said: 'Life is a cattle-grid.'?"

"I did."

"Who said: 'The Earth is a fly.'?"

"Me, I mean I."

"Who said: 'Silence is unruly.'?"

"Yours truly."

"*And* you said: 'To have is to be had.'"

"Really? Not bad!"

Drugtaker's Caution

"On high alert.

Don't try to insert."

He's Just a Chap
Who Can't Say Yes

"You call it a 'window of opportunity'.

Frankly, your suggestion is an importunity

That calls into question your sense of

propriety

And has wrecked our already fragile

friendship by an impiety."

Over-Reaction

"To call me 'Babe' was so unwise:

It irked me, seemed to patronise.

'Coochie-coo' I could have taken.

'Babe', though, has left me very shaken,

Implying I'd be specially happy

If I wore a baby's nappy

Over my bitty-bits and tummy,

And dribbled, gurgled, sucked a dummy!

Some, I know, are into this,

Soiling the nappy with their piss

And more - not *my* idea of bliss!

'Sausage' or 'Honey' I could swallow;

At 'Cherub' or 'Duckie' I wouldn't holler;

But *'Babe'*,oh no!! In your nursery pen

I never shall be 'Babe' again!

I'm packing the layette, Beloved.

As for the rattle, you can shove it!"

Knightsbridge Barracks

Super bodies - hang their expense.

The only problem: Basil Spence*.

*Sir Basil Spence designed the complex that is Knightsbridge Barracks.

Owls

I found him without wit.

I was not prepared to woo.

I asked him from my branch to flit.

I'm glad he's hooting you.